Memories and Miracles

Memories and Miracles

STORIES AND REFLECTIONS
ON RUSSIANS FROM AN
AMERICAN MISSIONARY

Mary Theresa Webb

ISBN: 1974267873
ISBN 13: 9781974267873
Library of Congress Control Number: 2017912288
CreateSpace Independent Publishing Platform
North Charleston, South Carolina

To all our grandchildren, both Russian and American.
May each of you make a difference to keep the peace and heal the sick.

Contents

Prologue: Motivation

THE TIMING TO SHARE MY stories seems appropriate, especially with current Russian-American relations perilous and strained. My acquaintance with the Russian people developed through many short-term trips to Russia from 1989 to 2005. They're now my friends and not my enemies. I understand their strengths and weaknesses—some of their weaknesses have led them to be content with the kleptocracy they now find themselves in. Later, I will reflect more about current circumstances for both America and Russia. But first I want to share my stories and impressions from my numerous missionary trips.

Why Russia? The simplistic answer is this: God sent me. In fact, God embedded in my heart words from this hymn and these scriptures that formed the calling to follow where I believe he has led and empowered me:

> "Here I am Lord.
> Is it I, Lord?
> I have heard you calling in the night.
> I will go, Lord, if you lead me.
> I will hold your people in my heart."

And he said,
Go and (show mercy).

Luke 10:37 NIV

Build up the ancient ruins,
…raise up the former devastations;
…repair the ruined cities,
the devastations of many generations.

Isaiah 61:4 ESV

Do justice, and to love kindness and to
walk humbly with your God.

Micah 6:8 RSV

Acknowledgments

WHEN I FIRST BEGAN WRITING down my stories, I created a website with the title of this book. However, the contents of the website under my name disappeared into cyberspace. Since I didn't want to lose the stories, I wrote down as many of them as I could remember. These recaptured stories and musings formed the basis for this book.

I'm grateful to the Pittsburgh Leadership Foundation and the members of the Coalition for Addictive Diseases for undertaking what first began as the Russian Project in 1992. During the years from 1989 to 2005, the name of the Russian Project under the Pittsburgh Leadership Foundation, became Theodosian Ministries, because a Russian Orthodox sect by that name took care of the needs of the sick and poor in the 1880s. Since our ministry with Russians was designed to help those with the disease of addiction, the name change seemed appropriate for our recovery ministry in both Russia and Romania. But when the ministry expanded to Honduras in Central America, Egypt, and then Kenya, Jay Geisler, a board member in Pittsburgh, thought another name change would be appropriate. Global Addiction Recovery Leadership and Learning (GOAL) registered as a not-for-profit with the Commonwealth of Pennsylvania in 2002. However, in 2013, the GOAL board decided that GOAL's working title should be Global Addiction Recovery Partners because that's what we were about—partnering with churches and missionaries in East Africa and Eastern Europe.

I'm grateful for the many GOAL missionaries who felt called to join a GOAL team for the recovery ministry in Russia: Rev. Bob Hughes, Rev. Kevin Fisher, Rev. William Teska, Bruce and Helen Dolph, Dr. Andy Spickard, Dr. Darv and Carol Smith, Tom Nega, the Rev. Dave Else, Carol Shank, Dr. Wes Sowers, Dr. Ken Thompson, Dr. Jean LaCour, and others, including members of the International Substance Abuse and Addiction Coalition (ISAAC), joined hands with Pam Brunson, Chris Saunders, and many outstanding Russian colleagues to provide hope for addiction recovery in Russia. Bob and his wife, Barbara, undertook the responsibility for the project in Romania, working with missionary Floyd Frantz. Most of those who have been missionaries or team members have shared their personal stories of recovery while serving as missionaries or gave of their professional time as addiction experts.

There have been several times in GOAL's history that we wanted to quit, but somehow with trust in God and perseverance, we managed to keep going. A three-year grant under the PEPFAR New Partners Initiative for Kenya brought GOAL to a new level. In a subsequent move to Lancaster, once again we started over with a bare-bones budget. With the opiate epidemic close to home, GOAL turned its attention to facilitating the same kind of workshops in the United States that we had facilitated in Russia. This time, with a team of local pastors and physicians, who were also addiction professionals, GOAL forged ahead. However, like OPORA, sustainability of GOAL's mission depends on a strong board, advisers, and the proven ability to raise the needed capital in order to continue. As throughout its history, GOAL will need to depend on God as well as commitment of staff. Not only the sustainability of programs we have initiated in other countries but also our own sustainability continues to be a challenge.

PART I

Nuclear-Arms Race

Prophetic Concern

But you have planted wickedness,
you have reaped evil,
you have eaten the fruit of deception.
Because you have depended on your own strength
and on your many warriors,
the roar of battle will rise against your people,
so that all your fortresses will be devastated...when
mothers were dashed to the ground with their children.

HOSEA 10:13–14 NIV

WITH MUSHROOM CLOUDS LOOMING AND radioactive fallout about to descend, I acted. If one person could make a difference, I would try.

The time period was the 1980s. But the seeds were planted earlier in my life than that, beginning on that infamous day, August 6, 1945, the day our nation dropped a nuclear bomb on Hiroshima, then three days later, Nagasaki. Several days later the Japanese surrendered and World War II ended. Shortly thereafter, an undeclared war between the United States and the former Soviet Union began. Although no shots had been fired, the Cold War—as it was called then—lasted forty years until the

1990s. A period of détente followed. The undeclared war resumed when Putin became president. This animosity between two world superpowers has been calculating and oppressive, each country set on becoming the greatest superpower and dominating the world.

When Japan surrendered, our family had been vacationing in a cottage on an island off the coast of Maine. I remember our reactions—the adults applauding while tuned to our lone radio and we children leaping and shouting. My friend Jane and I climbed over rocks along the shore until we reached the summer church where we rang the church bells. We found several firecrackers left over from the Fourth of July and set them off on the rocks in front of our cottages.

Little did we know then that those first mushroom clouds of devastation from the two nuclear bombs that brought the Japanese to their knees would overshadow our lives for the next seventy years. The stockpiling and testing of new generations of nuclear weapons would lock us into a nuclear-arms buildup race with the Soviet Union and to a proliferation of countries building their own nuclear arsenals.

Located in the basement of our house in the woods outside of Pittsburgh, we had a corner for a bomb shelter and had stockpiled it with a homemade Geiger counter and plastic and tape to seal doors and windows. Others built underground bomb shelters. Any one bomb, detonated in the atmosphere, would destroy us all. Carl Sagan, of the Union of Concerned Scientists, and Helen Caldicott, of the Physicians for Social Responsibility, warned there would be no survival for anyone from a nuclear war. Nuclear winter would result. I joined with other concerned educators and formed Educators for Social Responsibility. Concerned clergy groups grew. Clergy of all denominations became involved.

We even became afraid of nuclear power plants. When radiation leaks at Three Mile Island and Chernobyl occurred, we believed our fears were justified.

As an environmental educator, I realized that the greatest environmental disaster would be the destruction of the earth through nuclear winter. At a special training session at the National Cathedral in Washington, DC, representatives from the National Security Council showed a group of us laity and clergy from the Episcopal Church different nuclear warheads. Two men explained the nuclear war-game strategies, hours and days spent in closed-door sessions attempting to figure out what their Soviet counterparts were plotting. We read the Catholic bishops' pastoral letter on the morality of the nuclear-arms race. Gradually, heretofore complacent and compliant Christians like me became peace activists.

Prophetic Action

I GATHERED FOLKS IN MY living room for coffee to warn them about the dangers of the nuclear-arms race. I joined demonstrations and peace walks. We peace activists went to Washington to appeal to Congress.

Meanwhile, there were several close calls to starting a nuclear war. One occurred when the White House received an alarm that the Russians had launched a nuclear warhead. Fortunately, cool heads prevailed in the Situation Room not to retaliate. By fact-checking it was determined that the supposed launch was false news.

Our Episcopal Church Diocese formed a Peace Commission, and the members of our commission determined that we would practice conflict resolution, include in our deliberations those who didn't agree with us, and do what we could to help resolve conflicts around the world. One member of our committee decided to host students from war-torn Ireland where Protestants and Catholics had been fighting each other.

Teresa Heinz (now Kerry) phoned me, asking for my help in starting a Pennsylvania chapter of Peace Links. Senators' wives, led by Betty Bumper, the wife of then Senator Dale Bumper, pledged to start Peace Links branches in every state. Pennsylvania's began under my leadership of an enthusiastic group of women in Pittsburgh, who eventually went on to initiate lesson plans in peacemaking in area schools. When the dissolution of the former Soviet Union and détente with the West solidi-fied, Peace Links' efforts disbanded.

Meanwhile, one day in 1988, my fellow peacemaker and friend Shirley Woolaway and I learned about a special tour group called Peace Odyssey.

Praying and Pleading

Lead me from Death to Life, from Falsehood to Truth
Lead me from Despair to Hope, from Fear to Trust
Let Peace Fill our Heart, our World, our Universe.

A PRAYER FOR PEACE

WE GRANDMOTHERS IN BOTH THE former Soviet Union and the United States had been praying this prayer. We prayed in churches. We prayed in monasteries. We prayed in our homes on our knees. We pleaded with God, "Save your people, Lord, from radiation death and sickness, from the devastation of the earth."

On my first trip to the former Soviet Union, I met a young nun who had joined a convent to pray for peace.

American and Russian praying

Besides nuns, Russian grandmothers kept candles lit in Orthodox church buildings, buildings that had long since been denuded—their crosses removed—and turned into swimming pools, factories, and museums.

Laypersons left without clerics found ways to keep the faith alive, holding weekly services for friends and neighbors behind closed doors in their apartments or in nearby woods. Leading two lives, one public and one private, they hid their treasured icons and crosses and prayed for an end to Communism. During family worship times, icons and Bibles were retrieved from closets and other hiding places. They taught their children the ancient prayers of their ancient faith. Thousands of *babushkas* (grandmothers) had their grandchildren secretly baptized. Tragically, many of their hidden icons and other religious art were sold on street corners during Communist years. After the years of Perestroika, retired persons, now living on inadequate pensions, trying to live in the aftermath of Communism, had to sell their once secret treasures in order to survive. Sometimes, members of their parishes found them, repurchased them, and donated them to a parish church.

Marie Elizabeth and her husband had kept their traditional Russian Orthodox beliefs in this way.

Marie Elizabeth

Andre, a psychiatrist and research scientist, introduced me to his babushka, Marie Elizabeth, and his mother, Emma, on one of my early trips to Moscow. I had dinner with them in their three-bedroom apartment.

Marie Elizabeth hadn't ventured outside much from her room in their apartment during all the years of Communism. Perhaps she was still afraid because her late husband had worked as an accountant for a state-operated firm and had refused to join the Communist party; nor did he take the oath of allegiance required by his trade union. Instead, they prayed and taught their grandson his catechism along with his school lessons. Nor did the ban on Christianity stop Emma, their daughter. With my encouragement, she wrote about her trials living under Communism. After the Revolution, she started an orthodox school for children in an abandoned building as well as a publishing house. She lost her job as an English professor at the Moscow University, and her son, Andre, lost his position at the state-funded alcohol research institute. With no research to occupy his time, he contemplated moving to America.

PART II

First Impressions of Russians

Peacemaking Journey

Peace banner

MY FIRST TRIP TO THE Soviet Union took place in 1989, a year after the millennium celebration of Russian Orthodox Christianity. That year, Shirley Woolaway and I were able to join the next Peace Odyssey trip led by Dick Rodes, a retired Baptist pastor, and his wife, Jean. Our tour group included individuals from all over the United States—peacemakers like ourselves—who aspired to meet Soviet people.

Jean and Dick had been leading tours to meet the residents of the "evil empire"[1] since the early eighties. Shirley and I were the 401st and 402nd peace pilgrims with Peace Odyssey Tours who wanted to meet face-to-face with Soviet citizens. Each of us made conscious choices to set aside all preconceived notions of the Russian people, to listen to their human stories, and to become acquainted. Our group carried personal statements of a need for peace as well as a quilt made by American schoolchildren. I purchased Bibles and had each person in our group put a few Bibles in his or her suitcase, just in case some suitcases might be opened and Bibles confiscated by customs officials.

Our group flew into Helsinki, Finland in October. There we boarded a ship to Tallinn, Estonia. Besides our small tour group of Americans, Soviet and Estonian citizens with their multicolored striped cloth suitcases, loaded with newly purchased clothes, carrying TVs and other electronic devices, stood and sat around us.

When our ship docked, with my heart in my throat and my hands perspiring, I handed over my passport and visa to the waiting customs official in his booth. Miraculously, that day he didn't examine our tour group's suitcases, nor did he open the packages and bags of the other Soviet citizens and local Estonians. They made it through customs with all their foreign purchases as did we with our Bibles.

Anticipatory independence from the Soviet Union permeated our time in Estonia before we boarded our train to Moscow. In an upper room, a group of proud citizens shared their newly written constitution created during a Baltic Assembly on May 13–14, 1989. As we were to discover in our travels, many others were preparing for the time when Communism would not dominate their lives. Dick Rodes shared with us their desire was to create a dynamic order so that they might take their rightful place in the world family of nations.

We boarded the train for Moscow as dusk was beginning to fall. From our train windows, we watched scene after scene in fast-forward motion of the bleak snow-covered countryside. Denuded trees and drab buildings flashed into occasional view. Shirley recalled arriving in Moscow to gray skies and snow-covered streets and sidewalks. One of my first purchases was a pair of Russian snow boots.

After turning over our passports and visas at the front desk of the Intourist hotel, we located our rooms on the fifteenth floor. Our room smelled of stale cigarette smoke and was as gray and dingy as the skies. Sleeping-room areas were closed off by glass doors from where the elevators where located. Meals were served communal style for us tourists in a separate dining room on the first floor.

We stayed in our hotel only to sleep and for two meals a day while being carefully guarded by our communist guide/minder. Although Soviet citizens were forbidden by their government to visit Americans in Intourist hotels, no one stopped them from inviting us into their apartments. Dick's friend Nina gave no heed to the consequences of these protective restrictions and invited our tourist group for tea in their comfortable book-lined living room in a well-furnished flat, an oasis out of place with the crumbling building exterior.

Terry and Shirley with hosts

A Drunken Society[2]

AFTER SPENDING A FEW DAYS in Moscow, our group flew to Tbilisi, Georgia, where we were hosted for dinner at the home of Lili Marabishvili. We were not prepared for the feast spread out before us. The tables were put together to make a long banquet table and took up most of the adjoining rooms in a small flat (apartment). The two families who hosted us shared the same kitchen. The women of those two families had spent all day cooking and the men had brought out their homemade vodka and wine. They served us course after course of delectable pastries, meat, vegetable dishes, and cakes while the men toasted us and the young girls entertained us with singing and dancing.

As the evening wore on, our hostess, a physician, grimaced and stopped smiling. I knew the signs well. I watched her glare at her now drunk husband who had become the life of the party. As we were getting ready to leave, she beckoned me to come behind a curtain and pleaded with me to find a way for their son to come to the United States for schooling. I agreed to try.

"Could we visit a narcological center?" I asked her husband, the head of the Health Department in Tbilisi, as we said our good-byes. "*Kanyeshna* (of course)," he mumbled while we put on our shoes and coats. "*Zaftra* (tomorrow)."

The next morning, our physician host picked us up at our hotel and drove us in his automobile to the Narcological (Addiction Treatment) Center. The chief narcologist (addiction specialist) greeted us at the door and guided us on a tour through his facility. After the tour, we joined him, and some members of his staff seated around his conference table. He carefully demonstrated the elements of an assessment tool their staff used to determine the extent of chemical dependency, similar to many that we used in the States. As he explained the number of drinks that crossed the line between safe use and abuse that causes intoxication, our host physician interrupted, "Why I can drink more than that!"

Smart narcologist, I thought.

Afterward, we had another meal with more drinking and toasting. Shirley and I nodded to each other and told our host that we needed transportation to return to our hotel.

"Could we get a taxi?" Shirley asked.

"*Nyet* (no)," our wobbly host slurred.

He was insistent on driving us back to the hotel. We hesitated, but what else could we do? As Shirley and I sat together on the back seat, I whispered, "He's too drunk to drive!"

"Pray," she whispered back, clutching my hand.

Our drunk driver sped through the city streets, ignoring stoplights and careening around other vehicles. Only by God's grace did we arrive back to our hotel in one piece.

True to my word, when I returned to my apartment in Pittsburgh, I called my friend Larisa Mason. Larisa, a Russian American, had started a not-for-profit organization in Pittsburgh to place Russian children from an orphanage in St. Petersburg into American families. I told her about the Georgian physician's request for their son to come to school in America. She contacted her son's school principal. Because of their willingness, the Georgian physician's son, Peter, was invited to attend Shady Side Academy for six months. When Peter's father came to visit his son, he took Peter with his twelve-year-old friends to a bar and ordered beer for all of them. Needless to say, the next day he received a tongue-lashing in Russian from Larisa.

Lost and Found

AFTER LEAVING TBILISI, OUR GROUP flew to Belarus and then Leningrad. In every city, hosts and hostesses set up banquet tables in their crowded flats and treated us to scrumptious feasts with many toasts. We distributed the gifts we had brought at each stop and kept our roll of toilet paper handy. In turn, our hosts and hostesses gave us their prized possessions, *matryoshka* (nesting) dolls and lacquered boxes, from right off their shelves.

When we visited the museum of history and technology, the only exhibit in the museum was a wheelbarrow.

"Where are the other exhibits?" I asked.

"There are none," our guide replied. "We've lost our history. Everything we've been taught is false."

Shame, not pride, seemed to be the norm of the Soviet citizens we met in other cities where we journeyed in our attempt to break the barriers of hostility to become their friends.

Because we either took a train or an Aeroflot plane from city to city, we became acquainted with Soviet citizens. We chatted across the aisles with them on our plane rides; we in our attempts to speak Russian and they in their crisp British English or American slang they had learned from watching American movies on TV. We exchanged telephone numbers and addresses. We discussed the horrors of the fallout from Chernobyl and our mutual concerns about the dangers of nuclear weapons. On each flight, we applauded the pilots who walked through the plane on their way to and from the cockpit. Our stewardesses, middle-aged women with head kerchiefs, served us tea from samovars located at the end of the aisles.

We were busy getting to know one another in this way on our flight from Georgia to Belarus when the pilot announced all too soon that we were landing.

"No photos," our guide warned us. "Not allowed in airports."

While we waited for our luggage to arrive, I realized that I had left my purse on the plane. Elena, our guide, went back to the plane to ask the cleaning crew if they had found my purse.

She shook her head when she reappeared. "*Nyet.*"

She then checked with the driver of the bus that had brought us from the plane. My purse wasn't there either. She talked to an agent who promised to check around the airport again the next morning before our plane that had brought us departed.

When I arrived at my hotel room, I made a list of everything that I could recall that was in my purse: American dollars, some Russian rubles, half of my traveler's checks, prescription glasses, keys, a gold bracelet made for me in Jerusalem with the word *Shalom* engraved on it, a silver cross given to me by our Soviet hostess as I was leaving Tbilisi, some peace tokens, and an address book. Nothing else could be done except to turn the whole matter over to God. I prayed through my anxiety and disappointment about losing all the addresses of my newfound friends that I had collected on our flight. I closed my prayer that night by asking God to use the purse for his purposes and that whoever found it would have a need for its contents. I woke refreshed and began the process of replacing my traveler's checks that we all used back then instead of credit cards; fortunately, some were still in my fanny pack that I carried in my waist inside my clothes.

What a lengthy process I faced. First, it involved trying to contact American Express in Moscow and Leningrad. Putting telephone calls through sometimes took days, so it wasn't until we reached our last stop that I succeeded, which involved several days of perilous adventures. I wandered the backstreets looking for the American Express office and almost got run over by a bus. After I finally found the office, I was told to return the next day with my passport and to show it at a bank. At the bank, I waited in a long line for an hour. Eventually, clutching the precious replaced traveler's checks, I dashed back to our Intourist hotel just in time to meet the tour group as it was ready to board the bus that would take us to the airport for our Aeroflot flight to Finland, where we were to change planes for our flight to America.

After I had returned home, I replaced the prescription glasses and bought a new purse. I reminded myself not to get so involved with talking to fellow plane passengers the next time I traveled by air, that I didn't have time to check my carry-ons more carefully!

Two weeks after my return, I received a phone call from a PAN AM airlines official. He said that they had a package for me and could they deliver it to our apartment. To my astonishment, when I opened the door, in the deliveryman's hands was the purse that I thought I would never see again. I checked the contents with excitement. Everything was there as I had left it, including the money. Nothing was missing, except the silver cross, which had been in a zippered compartment. I knew then that the small silver cross had stayed in the Soviet Union for a purpose, to be a symbol of hope in the midst of the pain of disruption and change, a symbol that God had answered my prayer.

During that trip, I discovered that the Soviet people we encountered were hospitable and honest, and they were as eager to make friends with us Americans as we were with them. Their strengths of endurance, deep spirituality, native intelligence, and sense of humor had sustained them. As I share more of my stories, you'll come to know of their innate optimism and ingenuity. You will also discover that they have a tendency to fail to take personal responsibility and have a high tolerance for corruption and bribery. These traits, engrained in their years under Communism, have kept them locked under authoritarian regimes.

Our last night in Leningrad, we attended a play at the local theater. The play symbolized the breakdown of barriers between people groups— an appropriate ending to our peacemaking journey. And as our plane flew over Berlin on our return flight home, the Berlin wall was being broken down with hammers and axes by East and West Germans. East Germans, once lost behind the Iron Curtain, could now find their West German relatives.

A Russian Con Artist

WE HAD JUST RETURNED FROM an exhausting day of sightseeing when Dick knocked on our hotel door and asked if we wanted to see some paintings of an exceptionally fine young artist he had met on his last visit to Moscow. For us Americans, Russian artists and musicians were a cut above the stereotype of the violent-tempered Russians flying down on their horses from the steeps, with Tartar bloodthirsty revenge. Instead, we Americans esteemed Russian artists and musicians. We looked forward to meeting Alexi.

My first impression of the tall, slender dark-haired youth with the cigarette dangling out of his mouth was a vague sense of wariness. Notwithstanding my feeling, I looked at his paintings stretched out on the floor before me, and one particular one mesmerized me. It was a watercolor painting of a woman tottering under a street lamp with a bag beside her. She reminded me of some of the bag ladies I had been working with in the shelters of Pittsburgh. Around her was a red line.

"*Mother Russia*," explained Alexi.

Another painting depicted an icon of Christ.

"Are you a Christian?" I asked Alexi.

"Yes," he replied.

I bought *Mother Russia*. Another member of our group, Kay Saunders, was so impressed with Alexi's work she bought another one. When she returned to the United States, her colleagues at the university in Reno, Nevada, were also wowed with the painting she had bought. They decided to invite Alexi to visit and to sponsor an exhibition of his paintings.

Alexi had grown up and displayed his art on Arbat Street. He usually spread out his watercolors and oil pictures to sell daily to any passerby. In the 1980s, after Americans began to visit Moscow in increasing numbers, he had taken every opportunity to sell his paintings to them, to learn their language, and to bargain for American dollars and cigarettes. Sometimes he invited them to his flat, where he lived with his wife, an iconographer, and his son.

Two and a half years later, I met Alexi again. Kay had been true to her promise. Not only had she invited him to the United States but also had arranged to have the university where she was a faculty member provide a studio for him to paint. She had covered every detail of his stay, including seeing to it that he would have adequate health insurance. Meanwhile, Alexi had saved enough American dollars to purchase a plane ticket on the black market and had secured a passport and visa to the United States. When he landed in New York City, he called Dick. Dick hosted him for a week and then sent him on to his destination, via Pittsburgh and Minneapolis.

Alexi shared our small apartment space for three days, while we visited all the Pittsburgh sites. We talked about his country, his wife and child, and the perilous economic and political situation. He expressed concern for his son and his wife who could not buy simple walking shoes. Our sightseeing tour of Pittsburgh started in an elegant restaurant overlooking the city and ended at the art museum where we joined a special tour of the art gallery. Alexi showed those on the tour pictures of his paintings and even the docent was impressed. During lunch at a restaurant in a shopping center, he spread out his paintings on the floor, just like in Moscow. A young woman sitting next to us raised her hands in delight. Her mother explained that her daughter was injured in an automobile accident several years ago and was brain damaged. She could only communicate by facial expression and gesture. At the time of the accident, she, too, had been a budding young artist. She bought one of his watercolors, clapping her hands with delight. A crowd of people joined her, anxious to meet Alexi. A few of them also bought other canvases. By the time we left the restaurant, Alexi had sold several hundred dollars' worth of paintings. By the end of the day, he had sold his wife's icons as well.

American Express was our last stop so that he could change his precious dollars into safer currency. Then I put him on the Greyhound bus on his journey via Minneapolis to Reno, Nevada.

Kay called me several weeks later. "Where is Alexi?" she asked.

She contacted the minister he was to be staying with in Minneapolis. From him she discovered that Alexi had been living with an American girl he had met on Arbat Street in Moscow. She had introduced him to a commercial artist in America who saw an opportunity to use Alexi to attract tourists. So Alexi stayed with her, became her lover and a novelty for the tourists. He told everyone that he had no family in the Soviet Union. He told them he did not have to go home. But he phoned me to ask what he should do about Kay.

I asked him once again, "Alexi, are you a Christian?"

"Yes," he replied again.

"Are you baptized?" I pursued the subject.

"No," he replied.

I recalled one of our conversations in Pittsburgh about how difficult it was sometimes to be a Christian. I suggested he find a pastor to learn about what Christianity is all about! After he hung up, I thought about the bottle I had seen in his suitcase and his mood of depression. I also remembered my vague sense of wariness when I had first met him in Moscow. His "street smarts" were similar to the homeless addicts I had worked with on the streets of Pittsburgh. Some of them had conned me too.

Alexi had learned to survive in the Soviet Union, as he was now surviving in the United States with his paints and his bottle. Little did he know about honesty and commitment. He had never learned them on Arbat Street. He did not know that vodka was not the elixir of life but a brain-altering drug. The little he knew about Christianity was how to paint icons. He also knew it was popular with Americans to be a Christian.

PART III

Americans and Russians Address Alcoholism

Planting Family Recovery

Having had a spiritual awakening as the
result of these steps, we tried to carry
this message to others, and to practice
these principles in all our affairs.

THE TWELFTH STEP OF
ALCOHOLICS ANONYMOUS AND AL-ANON

"SHARING WITH ONE ANOTHER AND experiencing little sympathies"
signifies what 12-Step recovery from the disease of addiction is all
about—in any country. A Moldovan woman at a 12-Step meeting in
Kishinev expressed these sentiments to the first Americans to dare
to visit that city since the demise of Communism. Tanks lined the
streets. Gasoline was rationed. People gathered in cluster groups on
the sidewalks in front of empty stores. They bartered for food and
clothes.

Bartering

Often vodka bottles were pulled out of bags in exchange for food. Gypsy women roamed the streets. Alcohol consumption, on the increase in a country with a deteriorating political situation, undermined the very fabric of life.

After my first trip to the Soviet Union in 1989, I knew that I wanted to return on a specific mission. That mission became a reality in March 1991, when my mail contained a flyer from Creating a Sober World (CASW), a program of the Center for US-USSR Initiatives in San Francisco, California. For the past five years, individuals in recovery from their own alcoholism had been helping set up Alcoholics Anonymous (AA) groups throughout the Soviet Union. Now eighty such groups were registered with their headquarters in New York City.

The flyer urged interested twelve-steppers to join their travel team, whose purpose was to establish and support Al-Anon (family member support groups). I did not have enough money in my savings account to pay for the trip. The Gulf War was raging, and travel was particularly hazardous.

I prayed about whether or not I should make the trip, and the answer was a clear: "Yes. I will take care of you."

Within two weeks I received contracts for two writing projects that would cover the expense of the trip.

I began to pack.

My room looked like a cyclone-hit room. Around the suitcase that I was packing to take with me on my second trip to the Soviet Union lay packages and letters, food and sundry drugstore items: Band-Aids and aspirin, razor blades and stockings, M&Ms and chewing gum, sanitary supplies and toilet paper, Bibles and recovery literature. All paper products were scarce, even toilet paper. Sanitary napkins and disposable diapers were unheard of. I pondered just how few clothes I could get by with on this trip, because there was now such a need for the other items.

"Make sure you take something to wrap your gifts," our trip leaders said. "Soviet citizens don't appreciate being treated as charity cases. They would rather make do or do without."

I had almost forgotten the decorated department store plastic bags and the tissue paper. I proceeded to pack those items as well.

My doorbell rang. My friend Larisa asked me to take an invitation for her best friend, Tanya, from Leningrad to visit her that summer. We sat at the kitchen table as she carefully wrote down Tanya's name and telephone number.

"I am so worried about her," she revealed. "She writes that her husband drinks all the time. He says he has nothing to live for. Sometimes there are such violent arguments that her eight-year-old son leaves the flat for days at a time. She sounds so depressed."

My real purpose for this trip was to reach out to family members of alcoholics and to support the fledgling Al-Anon groups, and starting new groups in cities we would be visiting. It was Larisa's friend that I kept in my heart until we reached our last destination, Leningrad, now renamed St. Petersburg. I called Tanya as soon as we reached the hotel. Her husband answered and said that she could not come to the phone and that he would translate for her.

"How could I get through to her," I pondered, "without him sabotaging my efforts?"

I arranged for them to meet me in the lobby of the hotel the next evening.

She was beautiful! Yet, her eyes betrayed her fear. She carried a large bouquet of roses, a hallmark of Soviet hospitality and graciousness, to give to me. I handed her the invitation and letter from Larisa and then suggested that I wanted her to join me for dinner the next night, our last in the Soviet Union, and to attend a meeting with me. Fortunately, her husband, a sailor, had to go to sea the next day, so he declined. My prayers were answered. The next night Tanya came for the invited dinner with her son and a friend to interpret for her. I shared my concerns about her husband's drinking and my story. Others from our group joined me in explaining that sharing our stories and encouraging others who lived with those who had problems with alcohol was the reason for our trip. She thanked me, but said that her husband's drinking was not so bad now and declined to attend the meeting with us.

That summer, on her visit to Pittsburgh, I had an occasion to meet with Tanya again, this time over lunch in our apartment. Larisa had been giving her sage advice, building her self-esteem, and helping her to see the reality of how living with an abusive alcoholic was affecting her.

"I always felt that I was the one who was at fault," she said.

This time we talked at length about the disease of addiction, how it affected us spiritually, mentally, and physically. She agreed to telephone three of the family member group contacts I gave her when she returned home. The Sunday before she was scheduled to leave the United States, she was baptized in the faith of her mother country. Her new Russian Orthodox brothers and sisters in the United States showered her with their love and their gifts. Since her father was dead, she now had a new American godfather, Gregory, who promised to be her guide and to be the father figure in her new Christian life.

Armed with the assurance of God's grace and God's protection, she returned to the Soviet Union. There she made the telephone calls she had promised to make. Currently, she is a gallant, vibrant fighter for free-dom in her country—freedom from the devastating effects of alcohol on the lives of her countrymen and women. Vodka, the national drink, and wine, often homemade, were part of the social fabric of society. The Communist government had rationed and distributed vodka to soldiers, sailors, and farmers as rewards. Vodka had been a tool used by the party to keep people submissive and subservient.

CASW friends on train

On the CASW trip, there were thirteen of us, all in recovery for our family disease of alcoholism and another drug addiction. Men and women from AA and its Al-Anon companion group greeted us at the train station in Moscow by handing us bouquets of roses. Our Russian guide, Alena, joined us for most of our trip through the Soviet Union, leaving her two children Ala, eight years old, and Dasha, eight months old, in the capable care of her mother. In Kiev, she presented to their Al-Anon meeting her handwritten Russian copy of the Twelve Steps and Twelve Traditions. She shared her experiences about learning to live with her husband, who had the alcohol addiction disease with its frequent relapses. She met him when he was hospitalized after many times being sent to forced labor camps. While in the hospital, a visiting person in recovery from the United States had introduced him to the AA program. Alena had been helping him start a meeting in their two-room flat.

After being with our family recovery group for two weeks, Alena realized she could not work her husband's program for him and needed to continue to work on her own growth and self-care.

The Kiev meeting took place in a room at a local narcology center. In Moscow, one meeting we attended was in the basement of a building in a hospital; another, in a rented hall. Other meetings were in homes where there was space big enough to seat us all. Particular highlights of the meetings were holding hands and saying the Serenity Prayer in two different languages.

When our group reached Kishinev, Moldova, we found that we were the first Americans in that city for four months. Salva, a young physician trained in a treatment center in Oregon, had returned to Kishinev to start his own treatment center for abused children. Sixty percent of them suffered because of the alcohol addiction of one or both parents. Sasha led us American twelve-steppers as we journeyed by trolley and foot to the recovery meetings being held at his new center. The groups, established the prior year, were floundering and needed the reassurance of their American guests. Alcoholism was on the increase in that country, with the deteriorating political situation and women often found themselves living in abusive situations with nowhere to turn for help.

I sat next to a twenty-one-year-old dark-haired young woman. She had that scared look on her face as we began the meeting, slouching down in her chair as if to try to remain hidden. Finally, after all of us had shared, she got up the courage to speak.

"My husband is on alcohol and drugs. I gave up everything to put him through school. He reads the Bible with me. He tells me that alcohol and drugs help him philosophize. Sometimes he is violent."

We encouraged her to take care of herself. At the end of the meeting, we exchanged gifts. Her face beamed.

"What is lacking in our society" said one of our hosts, "is this ability to share our problems with one another and experience that we all have similar problems."

Everywhere we went, fledgling recovering alcoholics and their family members wanted us, the Americans, to tell them how to work the program. Often just sitting in a circle and sharing with one another was a new experience for them. They had remained isolated one from another, frightened to talk because of the KGB. Joint decision-making, or "group conscience" as 12-Step recovery groups call it, was a foreign concept. One or two persons often monopolized the fledgling groups and made all the decisions. They desperately wanted any literature and offered to translate anything we gave to them into Russian. We made ourselves available. We made the connections. We shared openly and honestly. We expected miracles to happen and they did. We provided hope in the midst of chaos and confusion. Our Soviet friends now wanted us American recovery missionaries to keep "coming back."

Even though we weren't ready to return to the United States, there came the day when we had to say good-bye to our new friends. Once our suitcases had cleared customs, we waited for the announcement that it was time to board the plane. Our leader, who was waiting in the seat beside mine, turned to me and said, "Terry, how would you like to lead these recovery groups in the future?"

"No way!" I replied, shaking my head vehemently.

But God overruled me. The next twenty-six years, that's exactly what he had planned for me to do.

Russian American Collaborations

Lord, make us instruments of your peace.
We know that it is only in your presence
that we can gain the serenity
to have the courage to change the world
and gain the wisdom to make a difference.

Adapted from Reinhold Niebuhr's Serenity Prayer

A PLAN EVOLVED OVER THE next few years: to develop Russian/American collaborations on alcohol and drug-prevention programs. No sooner had I arrived back to my home in Pittsburgh than I received a phone call from a priest in New York, Father Luis Dolan. Father Dolan had been instrumental in joint conferences at the Danilov Monastery in the Conference Hall of the Department of External Relations of the Moscow Patriarchate in 1989 and 1990. Father Dolan had headed the American delegation. The conferences became known as Soviet-American Conferences on Alcoholism. He had heard about me from our CASW tour leader from California.

"At our second conference in Moscow," he began, "I met Father Irinarch Grezin. He wants to bring over a delegation to visit Baltimore, New York, Washington, and other cities to learn about prevention and the development of alcoholism in the family, would you be interested in hosting them in Pittsburgh?"

I approached the Coalition for Addictive Diseases (COAD), a program of the Pittsburgh Leadership Foundation, and asked if they would be interested in hosting the group. We met and enthusiastically decided to involve the Russian Orthodox churches and local communities where they were located when the delegation came to Pittsburgh.

When the delegation arrived in the winter of 1992, we met Father Irinarch, his bishop, and a young psychiatrist, Dr. Andre Vedeniapin. During their stay in Pittsburgh, they were wooed and treated royally by Russian Orthodox priests, their wives, and parishioners. After touring other cities, the delegation decided to return to Pittsburgh before going back to Moscow. Apparently, during their first visit, we had captured their hearts.

After members of COAD and the Russian delegates were seated around a table at the headquarters of the Pittsburgh Leadership Foundation, Father Irinarch spoke.

"We have chosen the Pittsburgh Coalition to help us set up a rehabilitation program for alcoholics in my church."

Flattered, we agreed to consider the idea, but first COAD wanted to visit them in Moscow.

"What are your first needs?" Tom Nega, the chair of COAD asked.

"We need to develop a structure for our Orthodox Temperance Society," Irinarch responded, "and to hold joint seminars here and in Russia."

COAD agreed to send a team for the first seminar in the fall.

Even though I had some reservations about their Temperance Fellowship, as they called themselves, and the bottles of vodka I spied in their luggage, the members of the Pittsburgh Coalition chose a team to go for the first seminar to be held at Father Irinarch's church in Moscow that fall.

After collecting literature and finding suitcases large enough to carry our newsprint and Magic Markers, Father David Else from COAD, Fran Tarkett from Duquesne University, and I were ready to meet their challenge. I was off on my third trip for more adventures in this newly reborn country. From the Sheremetyevo International Airport, we were taken directly to the Orthodox Church of the Icon Mother of God, Joy and Consolation.

First, we managed to climb over piles of bricks being used by workmen to turn the building back into a church worship center, that had been recently dedicated back to God from the shoe factory it had been turned into under Communism. Fran led the assembled clerics and narcologists through a strategic planning process during the week. By the end of our sessions, we had covered every wall space with newsprint.

In between our training sessions, we visited Hospital #17, where a Caron Center American-model thirty-bed treatment center named

"Recovery" had started. Since 40 percent of the population in Moscow had been involved in some form of government or military project, many of them were now unemployed. In other parts of Russia, the unemployment rate was even higher. Vodka had become the unemployed's way of dealing with massive changes in their society. The Russian Orthodox churches being renovated were to become the center for all charitable work, even though the Moscow government was suspicious, as they had recently fired Dr. Droslov, who had been with the Moscow Health Department. He then joined Father Irinarch's Temperance Society.

Meanwhile, the new members of the Al-Anon group we had started the year before asked us to come and speak. Since we were the "experts," the assembled group wanted us Americans to tell them what to do.

"I'm here for me," I replied, "to share my experience, strength, and hope."

After that trip, our collaborations continued. Dr. Vedeniapin returned to Pittsburgh for on-site training at one private and one public treatment facility the following year. Meanwhile, he had broken away from Father Irinarch's Temperance Society and started his own charity. I returned to Moscow to help him write a proposal to the US Agency for International Development (USAID). On my return trip, I carried in my luggage Soviet-made knitting needles requested by Peter Hagerty of Soviet/American Woolens.

"My Moscow colleague has knitting needles made by her children's coop. Could you bring them back?" Peter had asked.

By that time, I had become a big supporter of his endeavor, purchasing his "Peace Fleece" yarn that blended wool from his Maine-raised sheep with wool from Soviet-raised sheep to knit sweaters for myself and hats and mittens for my grandchildren. Of course, I agreed. By then, I had been purchasing and bringing back with me Russian dolls, lacquered boxes, and tree ornaments to sell at yard sales and programs to support our efforts.

Peace Fleece partners

Selling Russian crafts

"What's in that suitcase?" a customs official asked. Andre, who had accompanied me to the airport that day, responded in Russian. Whatever he said must have satisfied the customs official because he allowed my suitcase to pass through.

Meanwhile, COAD was reevaluating its relationship with Irinarch's Temperance Society. So, when an invitation arrived to attend an international conference hosted by the Moscow University Medical School's Research Department, Tom Nega and I decided we would register. Drs Wes Sowers and Ken Thompson, both psychiatrists who had been attending our Russian project meetings, also expressed interest in attending the conference.

After we had purchased our nonrefundable plane tickets, I received notice that the conference had been canceled.

"But we have paid for our tickets," I e-mailed the conference organizer.

"Then we'll plan our own conference," she replied.

She met us at the airport and took us to her flat.

"You'll stay here," she announced. I looked around the small flat. There didn't seem to be enough rooms or beds—including the usual couches that Russians used for sitting or sleeping. Where would I sleep? Where would she? I hardly knew the three young men who were with me, let alone share a bed or even a room with any one of them.

As if to answer my thought, she said, "My husband and I are moving in with my sister."

"Then I'll get a room at a hotel, and the men can stay here," I added.

"I'm so sorry," she said. "Our physicians have not been paid for three weeks."

After sharing a meal prepared by our hostess, the three men, one with my large suitcase on his head, walked me over to my hotel, several blocks away.

After three days of improvised workshops, the four of us traveled by train to St. Petersburg (formerly Leningrad) and found lodging at the Petersburg Religious Academy (seminary). Our goal was to take a day to see historic St. Petersburg before our scheduled flight to return to Pittsburgh.

The next day was Sunday. Traditionally the doors of the seminary opened on Sunday after the midday meal so that the homeless could be invited to dine on any of the leftover food. We walked past the waiting line to get into the dining room as we were leaving for the airport.

"Where is your luggage?" I asked Ken Thompson.

"I left my suitcase and all my clothes."

He motioned to those standing in line patiently waiting for their turn to eat the only meal they would probably have for a week.

"They need them more than I do."

OPORA's Birth

"Bri-n-ng"

"Yes, who's calling?"

"My name is Pam Brunson," my caller announced.

"I'm a missionary with the Associate Reformed Presbyterian Church, and your name was given to me as someone who could help with the alcoholism problem in Russia. I'm home on furlough, but I need help organizing a seminar on substance abuse in cooperation with the Ministry of Health for Russian nationals and train professionals and church leaders in Christian recovery. Could you help?" she asked.

Pam, a former psychiatric nurse, found when she first arrived in Russia in 1996, a terrible epidemic of alcohol addiction. Forty percent of Russian men and 17 percent of Russian women were suffering from addiction to alcohol. Smoke from cigarettes permeated every building. Teenagers on heroin hung out with one another on their way to an unpleasant death. Abandoned children sniffed solvents.

"Why me?" I asked.

"Because I'm here in the United States for a year, but Irina Yakubova, who ably runs the Moscow-based Social and Cultural Alliance, has asked for help with facilitation of a seminar in my absence."

I'd been going back and forth with teams to Russia to help with the alcohol addiction prevention and treatment for the past six years. I thought immediately of my Christian friends and colleagues in the newly formed International Substance Abuse and Addiction Coalition (ISAAC), birthed at a conference in Florida hosted by the NET Institute. *Maybe some of them would be interested in being on a missionary training team.*

I contacted Darv and Carol Smith. Darv, a physician, and his wife Carol were running the Youth With a Mission (YWAM) school of addiction studies in Switzerland and said they could be available. Next, I contacted Dr. Andy Spickard Jr. of Vanderbilt University who had just written an important book on prevention. He and his wife also joined the team. Jean LaCour with her NET Institute certificates and evaluation forms in her luggage, and the rest of us, along with the books and pamphlets we carried, left the United States in September 1997 and met each other in Moscow. We arrived on one of those dreary, rainy, cold days. Russians were preparing for a harsh winter, bundling up with sweaters, coats, hats, and wool socks to protect them from the arctic blasts that penetrated poorly insulated buildings. The heat had not yet been turned on.

After a short rest, we were driven to the Seventh Day Adventist Center where some professionals were gathered. Andy Howard of World Witness joined us there. After the one-day seminar, we boarded buses to take us to a sanatorium conference site in a wooded area, a two-hour ride from the city. Our bus carried a copier machine, projector, TV, and other office supplies and equipment needed for the training. A statue of a pair of broken swans guarded the entrance of what used to be resplendent government facility. Grayish-white drab buildings loomed behind the swan statues. The buildings housed a Soviet hospital for sick soldiers.

Broken swans

With the start of the seminar delayed, because someone had forgotten to bring toner and cartridges, we had a chance to explore the beautiful birch trees surrounding the buildings and walk to a nearby lake. One of the Russians with us explained that as the weather grew even colder, men came to swim in the lake.

"To prove their masculine virility," she told us.

Delegates, eighty-five pastors, and small group leaders from evangelical churches in the Moscow region as well as from St. Petersburg, Voronezh, Samara, and the Ukraine, hungered for information about what to do with the alcohol problems of so many of those in their new congregations being devastated by the addiction epidemic. We American and Russian specialists had divided up the lectures on topics we planned to cover each day. The afternoons and evenings were free to show the videos we had brought with us and to model 12-Step support groups. Every night we met individually with those concerned about their own drinking or to share their concerns about family members who were affected. Our group of six women met outside in a gazebo.

Group meeting

"I don't know what to do," one woman sighed. "When my son comes home drunk, he picks up furniture and dishes and throws them against the wall."

"I'd lock my door and not let him in," one woman said.

"I'd call the police," another chimed in.

"I've done that. The police locked him up until he sobered up and then released him. The law says he has a right to stay in our flat. I have to take him back. What can I do?"

His violence will just get worse, and there are no abuse shelters, I knew. My heart sank. *What could I say?*

Another woman shared that she had a plan to go to a neighbor's flat whenever her husband came home drunk.

"I don't argue with him," another said. "I say the Serenity Prayer, let go, and stay out of his way."

Because the Russian women were sharing, I didn't have to say anything. Thereafter, in our late-afternoon discussions and support group meetings, participants learned from each other how to take care of themselves when their relatives came home drunk.

Most of the participants in the seminar were new Christians who were seeking to build or rent buildings to start a church, or had secured a worship space, or were still meeting to sing gospel songs and pray in woods surrounding their towns and villages. One evening I joined such a group. Their songs floated up along with the smoke from their wood fires. I listened. Even though the words were unfamiliar, the tunes were not, and I could hum along. I wished that I could have packed up their fervor and enthusiasm to take back to my churchgoing friends.

That conference spawned a support program called *OPORA* (support) that grew exponentially between 1997 and 2002, training over one thousand people in substance abuse education through its courses and workshops. OPORA seeded a recovery worship service that met in their space and initiated Christian 12-Step support groups. In its first two years, sixty recovery groups were started in thirty-one cities—meeting wherever they could find a place.

Along with members of the Associate Reformed Presbyterian Church providing the lion's share of funding through dinners and appeals of Pam and her husband, Ron, members of ISAAC, Family Ministries International of California, the Net Institute of Florida, the MERV project of the Episcopal Diocese of Southern Ohio, and the GOAL Project of Lancaster, Pennsylvania (then in Pittsburgh) led OPORA trainings all over Russia and Ukraine.

World Witness missionaries follow a philosophy of coleadership, and such was the leadership of OPORA; Pam Brunson, the American visionary missionary, worked alongside Irina Yakubova, the Russian administrator.

Pam and Irina

Several times conflicts flared between the two women.

On one of my trips, Pam, Irina, and I were walking toward the nearest metro station. Out of the blue, Irina started lashing out at Pam with angry and derogatory words.

What was that all about? I wondered. Later in that visit, I had an opportunity to have a private conversation with Irina.

"I never know what the budget is!" she fumed. "She pops in here with all her new ideas. She trains all these people, but I've never been able to be one of those trained. How can I run an organization when I don't even have the basic skills?"

That conversation and others led me to initiate and commission several mission team members —Kevin Fisher and William Teska—to conduct midprogram assessments of the OPORA program. Their reports, one prepared in 2003 and another in 2006, were then sent to Ron and Pam Brunson and World Witness.

OPORA Catches Fire

By 1999, ALL-RUSSIAN TEAMS OF specialists, sometimes aided by American GOAL-sponsored teams of recovering individuals and addiction specialists, had trained 180 individuals representing nine denominations from thirteen cities in local addiction outreach ministries. In addition to facilitating pastor-training seminars in Moscow, Tyumen, Ufa, and Kazan, OPORA staff produced a series of radio broadcasts on Christian recovery and published five recovery resource books. The OPORA cooperation between denominations was called miraculous. The impetus for church members to set up treatment centers of their own led to new centers started in Izhevsk and interest from Novosibirsk, Zheleznogorsk, Khabarovsk, and Tver. 12-Step support groups blossomed in all these cities.

Along with addiction recovery willing Americans, I have been a grateful member of this amazing healing process in Russia and elsewhere. Besides Moscow and its environs, St. Petersburg, Cheboksary, Izhevsk, Novgorod, Sablino, and Samara are cities where I have traveled and trained. From my notes, photos, and articles that were written in the nineties, I have rich memories of missionary miracles.

When I first learned about Chris Saunders and her Miami Valley Episcopal Russian Network (MVERN) project founded by the Diocese of Southern Ohio, I contacted her. At the time, MVERN had a partner church, St. Nicholas, in Sablino, outside of St. Petersburg, and was helping their young priest, Father Nikolai, with his struggling social projects, such as a nearby women's prison, an orphanage, and other youth programs. Many of the youth, he had discovered, were into alcohol and drugs.

When Chris Saunders told him about our OPORA trainings, he, too, wanted a seminar. With Dr. Andy Spickard as my fellow trainer, we responded to his request and led a seminar at Tosno, near Sablino. Subsequently, after receiving a grant from MVERN, an all-Russian team from OPORA trained forty specialists on preventing addictions among children and teenagers. Those who were trained formed a Committee for Youth, which initiated a Year of Prevention in Tosno in 2003.

One of my lectures included the evolution of alcohol used as the blood of Christ in Christian worship. During my talk, I often shared my story of suffering and recovery. After the Tosno lecture, a young social worker came up to me; her blue eyes brimmed with tears. She took my hands in hers and said in careful English, "Thank you for coming to Russia. It means so much to us."

Russian teaching tools

Miracle at Volgograd

WILL ALL OUR BAGS AND boxes of books and literature be under the weight limit? Our Russian/American team of trainers held our collective breath. We had divided the luggage between us just in case. The attendant behind the Aeroflot ticket counter stamped our tickets, as the boxes and bags made it through and into the hands of waiting baggage collectors who put them on a large cart.

When we arrived in Volgograd, we collected our boxes and bags. Our host and hostesses had planned a boat ride on the Volga River and a tour of a memorial of the German victory over Russians in Volgograd during WWII. Huge statues and a depressing underground museum overwhelmed us and were a constant reminder to the new Russians that they had been humiliated and shamed—yet hovering over the memorial was a large statue of Mother Russia with sword in hand, reminding Russian visitors that Russia would once again be triumphant.

Mother Russia statue in Volgograd

The images of shelled buildings and empty tanks were daily reminders lest the Russian people forget that they would rise victorious to be great again.

Our participants for the five-day basic addiction workshop consisted of fifty recovering heroin addicts and their family members, psychiatrists, and clergy. Volgograd had become the gateway for heroin manufactured from the poppies grown in Afghanistan. One out of every seven persons had become addicted to heroin, and 90 percent of the population abused alcohol. A newly formed not-for profit called "Salvation" sponsored by sixty-five new congregations planned to start a prevention program. At first, the clergy were skeptical of the 12-Steps until Bob Hughes, our board member and seminary theologian, convincingly taught them how the step process of recovery mirrored the Christian way of life. I introduced my book, *Tree of Life*, now translated into Russian, to reinforce his talk.

On the last night, while we were celebrating another successful workshop, knowing that we were leaving hope that there was life beyond the pain of addiction, one of the pastors approached us.

"What can I do about my brother?" he pleaded with us. "He's in jail, being charged with stealing because of his addiction."

"Love him and pray for him, but don't enable him," we told him, reinforcing our teaching. "Start recovery support groups in your church."

Our Russian/American training team split into two groups and rode in two automobiles with our luggage for the return ride to the airport. I rode alone in a small Volkswagen Beetle with the workshop leader, while the rest of the team and luggage went off in a larger vehicle.

For a while, we followed the larger car, until our small car got swallowed in traffic and lost the lead car. At that point, my driver decided to take a back route to circumvent the traffic jam. Yet, weaving in and around large potholes took forever and slowed us down. My anxiety level reached its peak when we finally arrived back at the main road the other car had taken. We stopped at a railroad crossing that was under construction. The departure time of our flight loomed much too close for my comfort.

A workman at the tracks waved down our car. My driver got out. I leaned my head out the window.

"You can't cross here," he told us.

"How do we get to the airport?" I queried and panicked.

"There is another crossing farther down the tracks."

I prayed and pondered. *We'll miss the flight.* My heart sank.

Suddenly another automobile appeared out of nowhere on the other side of the tracks. A man got of the car, walked across the tracks, and leaned in to talk to my driver.

"I'm here to take your American guest to the airport."

"How...?" I asked.

"After I deposited the others with the American man at the airport, a voice in my head told me to come back this way to the train tracks."

The Salvation Army captain/driver had heard God's response to my plea. With gratitude in my heart to God, I arrived at the airport just as the rest of our team had checked in and the loudspeaker was announcing the departure of our flight.

Stranded in Samara

By 2005, I had made many trips to Russia with Katja Savina as my translator. We had been to Russian towns and cities all over Russia. A Nigerian missionary, Meshach Chujor, a physician, had heard about OPORA/GOAL workshops and trainings at an ISAAC conference. He wrote to ask if we could come to Tajikistan to help set up 12-Step groups.

I arranged with Katja to accompany me since Tajiks speak Russian, not English. Our only Aeroflot scheduled flights to Dushanbe, Tajikistan, where the training would be held, had to be flying from Moscow to Samara, Russia, where we would need to change planes. Even though we had planned to travel together, Katja had to postpone her departure for several days and urged me to fly on ahead.

When I arrived at the Samara airport, I couldn't find my Aeroflot flight to Dushanbe, Tajikistan listed on the departure board. With my paper ticket in hand, I located the ticket counter and thrust it under the agent's nose. "*Nyet (no),*" he said, paused, shook his head, and handed me back the ticket. "*Zaftra* (tomorrow)." I understood just enough Russian to realize there would be no more flights to Tajikistan from the Samara airport that day, and that I would have to come back tomorrow.

I panicked. I knew no one. I was all alone in a strange airport, stranded in the middle of Russia.

Outside snow began to fall. I could see no other buildings, except the two small terminals—one for incoming flights and the other, for outgoing. With my small Russian/American dictionary in hand, I approached several official-looking Russians for anyone who would listen to my uncertain verbal attempts to be understood. After several *Ya nye panimayus* (do not understand), I approached a Russian attendant who could understand my faltering Russian.

"You could find a room in a hotel in Samara," she responded in English, "or sit up there."

She pointed to the stairs. I thought staying in a strange hotel a mile away from the airport would not be a wise idea, so I lugged my suitcases up a flight of stairs to a small waiting room, found a chair to prepare for a long night's waiting vigil, and prayed.

Call someone, the thought came as I fingered the notebook in my travel pack where I'd written some Moscow friends' telephone numbers. I did not have a cell phone with me because it had been lifted from my backpack on the Moscow metro train. Seeing one stationary phone on a nearby wall, I dialed one of the phone numbers from my book. A Russian voice answered.

Ya nye panimayus for both of us. I hung up, "Help...Lord!"

Find the attendant; ask her to call came into my mind, so I located the same English-speaking attendant and asked to use her cell phone. I dialed Irina's number, knowing that she could understand me.

"I'm stranded and can't get a plane out until tomorrow," I haltingly managed, panic edging my voice.

"I have a Christian friend who lives in Samara; let me call her," Irina offered.

I waited about an hour, maybe two. Then someone tapped me on the shoulder. I looked up into the face of a young woman with a twinkling smile. She asked my name. I grasped her outstretched hand and silently said a prayer of thanks to my guardian angel.

"My name is Marina," she said in English as she shook my hand.

By now snow had covered fields and roads. Marina had to carefully drive her small car dealing with hazardous road conditions. I didn't see a snow plow anywhere. But she kept me answering questions about life in America while driving in the blizzard. My anxiety diminished as shapes of the city of Samara came into view. She parked her car in front of a non-descript gray apartment building, like so many communist-built build-ings—buildings now owned by their occupants. With my suitcase in one hand, she guided me with her other to the elevator just inside the front door. Wafts of garbage and mold almost overwhelmed me. The elevator rattled its way to the fifth floor where Marina's mother greeted us. On a table in the kitchen, a steaming cup of soup, some bread, cheese, and tomato slices enticed me.

While I ate, the three of us talked, Marina interpreting for her moth-er. After my hostesses arranged for me to tour their Hospice ministry the next morning, I yawned and excused myself to retire to my bed, a brown couch in a small room off the warm kitchen.

Bedroom in Samara

Hospice friends

The next morning Marina and the staff at the Hospice clinic proudly showed me their newly acquired facility, a building that Marina's church had purchased. She drove me back to the airport in time for my scheduled Aeroflot flight to Dushanbe, now listed to depart at 1630 hours. Teary-eyed, we said our good-byes. There I sat with the other passengers to wait. When an announcement in Russian came over the loud speaker, I collected my luggage and started toward the gate. But the other waiting passengers around me didn't move. Puzzled, I sought the friendly English-speaking attendant to ask her if the announcement had been about my flight. "Canceled." She shrugged as if this was a common occurrence. I told myself, *Even though Russians are used to driving in snow, planes may still not be able to fly*. Stranded in this airport again.

"When…?" I asked.

"The next Aeroflot flight returns to Moscow," she replied.

Exasperated, I thought, *Katja's ticket is for tomorrow. She'll know what to do*. I bought a new Aeroflot ticket, flew back to Moscow to spend the night, and met Katja at the Domodedovo airport the next morning. Together we were determined to travel to Dushanbe for our delayed workshop. Our hosts in Tajikistan hadn't given up—so neither would we.

When our next-day Aeroflot flight from Moscow arrived at the now familiar Samara airport, snow lay on the ground, but none in the air. We collected our suitcases at the arrival terminal, trudged through the fallen snow to the departure terminal, and looked at the departure board. No Aeroflot flights were posted—only one Tajik flight. "That flight is over-booked," the same attendant told Katja in Russian. We could see many Tajik men crowding around the narrow gate, shouting and trying to push their way through to the waiting airplane, like a long sausage standing on the runway. The attendant kept shouting, "*Khvatit* (That's enough)!" and pushing them back.

Katja wound her way through the crowd and spoke something in Russian to the attendant guarding the gate, pointing back to where I was standing in the rear of the crowd. I tried to listen as they conversed. Katja caught my eye and beckoned me to come forward. A stewardess ushered the two of us onto the plane before all the waiting men and sat us in the two front seats. Katja leaned over and whispered in my ear in English, "I said you were an important American diplomat who had to be in Dushanbe today."

I wondered which two Tajik men had been displaced on their way home from their menial labors in Moscow and which two wives would be disappointed when their husbands did not meet them at the arrival gate. Would they be angry that their seats were taken not by an important diplomat but an American and a Russian missionary trainer? We carried no diplomatic pouches, only suitcases with recovery literature in Russian to help those addicted to heroin. This American woman with the help of her Russian colleague had persisted in order to bring hope and make a difference.

When we finally arrived at the Dushanbe airport, Dr. Meshach Chujor was there to greet us. Women and children gathered around our fellow Tajik passengers. I wondered how many of the ones left behind in Samara would find their only comfort in snorting or injecting heroin.

Even though the workshop had to be postponed, twenty eager students were waiting for us when we entered the classroom. Katja did most of the teaching, as I still had not mastered the Russian language. Students learned from her about the 12-Steps, and we modeled how support groups work.

Tajik trainees

Before we flew back to Moscow, we attended a church service with the Chujor missionary family while the Tajiks celebrated Ramadan with their families. I thanked God that he had cleared the way for the Tajik men and women we had met and traveled with to now have hope of heroin addiction recovery.

OPORA's Demise

A CLEAR PLAN TO ACHIEVE self-sufficiency for OPORA never materialized, in spite of the rapid growth and impact that OPORA had all over Russia in its first five years and in spite of the conclusions of the midterm evaluations our GOAL team members provided. Pam Brunson, who had been the driving force behind OPORA, decided to join her husband as a missionary couple in Pakistan in 2007.

"What will happen to OPORA if you leave?" I had asked her earlier.

"It will die," she admitted.

In 2008, World Witness instructed Andy Howard, who was then a missionary in Wales, to sell the Moscow building that housed the OPORA staff. The building had been purchased with monies from an American donor in 2000. Because of their rent-free space, OPORA had not had to pay rent and had sufficient funds to keep operating, but with no accountability for how they ran their program. By then Irina ran OPORA without Pam Brunson's guidance. She did not have enough experience with the challenges of national partnerships and ongoing funding to keep OPORA going once the building was sold. She retired from her position and a new person took over. But without the stability provided through World Witness voluntary donations, OPORA died a tragic death.

Kevin Fisher, a priest who joined several of our mission trips, predicted in his midterm report he prepared for GOAL that any project such as OPORA needs a system of accountability to a board of directors and to be able to cultivate other funding sources. Aware of the lack of an effective Board and group of advisers, I started an Advisory Council for OPORA and introduced their Russian director, Irina, to the concept of fund raising. However, any incentive for Russian businesses to support charitable organizations did not prove fruitful. In the new Russia, donations that are made to charitable organizations come from questionable mafia sources and the Russian underworld. Most Russian Christian organizations, such as OPORA, naturally want to avoid funds coming from shady sources as well as not having to pay bribes. Yet, bribery has been accepted by some as part of doing business. Christian NGOs like the Social and Cultural Alliance that seeded OPORA face an uphill battle to stay afloat financially.

PART IV

Significant Factors

Special Friendships

RUTH RYLANDER

WHEN I FIRST HEARD RUTH Rylander speak at a Mennonite conference on peacemaking, she became my mentor, my friend, and my encourager. Ruth started her peacemaking ministry as a result of her pain at the loss of her daughter, Lynn, to leukemia. She and her husband had some precious moments together to share with Lynn before she died.

When Ruth began to speak against the nuclear-arms buildup and the need for peace in her role as a staff member of the Pittsburgh Presbytery, she was labeled a Communist sympathizer by the more conservative members of her congregation. When she lost her job, she kept on giving talks and starting networks of peacemaking groups in individual churches. As a result of her peacemaking efforts, 183 congregations had active peace groups.

Then, in 1989, she, too, developed leukemia.

"I wonder why peacemaking leads to the depths of peace in the midst of the suffering and pain of disease?" she and I would muse together on the phone. Suffering seemed to bring out the best in Ruth.

"The difference is what people can do about it" was her motto.

The year her domination presented her with a Peaceseeker Award, I was in the audience to cheer and, afterward, to pray for her healing, as she sought every medical means to defeat the progression of her disease.

Her award read as follows:

"She has followed the Apostle Paul in planting the Gospel of Peace in her own church, the churches of her presbytery and the neighboring presbyteries and in the whole Church. And we must water them."

And so she did until her death from leukemia.

Doggedly I continued as chair of the Peace Commission of the Episcopal Diocese of Pittsburgh, challenging our own conservative members and the military/industrial complex so ingrained in our American culture. I led seminars on Reconciliation and Conflict Resolution to bring peacemaking closer to home.

VALENTINA MOSKALENKO, MD

I met Valentina Moskalenko when she came for a University of Pittsburgh conference in 1990, shortly after I had returned from my first trip to Russia. The University of Pittsburgh planners of the conference asked for volunteers to help, and I offered. Little did I know at the time that my assignment to drive Dr. Moskalenko from her hotel to and from the conference would be the beginning of a lifelong professional and personal friendship.

On our very first ride together, she turned to me and asked,

"Do you know where I can find information on Codependence?"

A colleague and I had been designing a *Codependence in Family Systems Assessment Guide*. I told her about our work. During the breaks in the conference, we squeezed in opportunities to discuss differences in affected families in our country and hers.

Both in Pittsburgh and in Moscow, we continued to meet and share. She thus became a cherished Russian friend and collaborator for our validated assessment tool. Many of my professional books ended up on her shelves and became the basis for her further work and counseling in Moscow.

When I was in Moscow, we attended family support groups together. After meetings, she sometimes invited me to her flat. While riding the metro together, we would discuss the new Russia that was being born in her country. *Would Russia become a socialist democracy?* we wondered.

"Democracy is messy and has its share of problems," I mussed as the metro train rattled along.

"But it's better than it was before," she replied optimistically.

When we reached our destination, her flat, and had removed our shoes, the first thing I noticed was that one room of Valentina and her husband's flat had been turned into a greenhouse. Seedlings peeked out of small pots of all sizes and shapes crowded together on any flat surface and covered all available spaces.

"For our *dacha* (summer home)," she explained. "You Americans don't know how much it means to us to have ownership of a dacha on our own plot of land. We've now grown just enough vegetables to see us through the winter."

Although she was now sixty years old and her husband had retired from his engineering job, they had to survive on her meager fifty-dollars-per-month salary she received from the state-supported addiction research institute where she still worked three days a week. Because of the dire economic conditions since the fall of Communism, their joint

government-supported pensions had been cut in half and the Russian ru-
ble continued to be devalued.

Later on, during one of our visits, she proudly told me that she had
her own radio show. "Family members call in—I get so many of them."

"One of my clients who I have been counseling spent the whole hour
of our last session crying on my shoulder. So much pain, so much suffering," Valentina sighed.

"Yes, and it takes longer to heal for codependent family members than
it does for the actual person who has the disease of addiction," I replied.

We talked. We shared. We grew to love one another. On one of my
visits, I brought bulbs to plant in her new garden; on another, I learned
that she was in the hospital with heart palpitations. Since I, too, suffered
in a similar way, I asked if I could pray with her. "I'm so scared," she said. I
prayed with her for healing. She had debated whether or not to go to Israel
for a special procedure, but after our time of prayer, she was well enough
that a pending trip to Israel for surgery was no longer necessary.

However, by 2011, Valentina did have some heart repair work done.
Today, she has become a popular author, radio, and internet celebrity and
now has enough money to live on. But growing beautiful roses gives her
the greatest pleasure.

KATJA SAVINA

Katja Savina became another special friend. For many years she had been joining our mission-team trips as our Russian translator/trainer. Besides interpreting for us Americans, she also lectured and shared in every city that we visited. With our support, she received her international certification as an addiction counselor and started her own treatment center, Zebra. Zebra has been functioning for eighteen years primarily on private donations, but the last three years with a Moscow government grant in payment for referrals from the Moscow state medical services.

Meeting at Zebra

On one of my visits, I taught a class of Ethics for Addiction counselors; on another, a class on smoking cessation. With her by my side, we held several round-table discussions with other Russian addiction professionals and planted the seeds for an all-Russian addiction professional organization. However, that effort floundered, but has now been revived.

Katja, a devout Russian Orthodox believer, has written several books. Her witness has been responsible for convincing the patriarch that the 12-Step spiritual way to recovery was acceptable.

Katja came to the United States as a guest of the National Association of Addiction Treatment Providers in 2006. We have kept in communication since then, and we exchange e-mails when she isn't busy helping those suffering from the disease of alcohol or heroin addiction.

The Vedeniapins

Emma and Andre

Andre Vedeniapin and his mother, Emma, remained special friends for many years.

Traditionally, a son or daughter lives with his or her parents until they're married. However, when Andre married, he and his new bride, Julia, had to move in with his mother and grandmother. Although Julia was a successful children's illustrator, her employers had not been able to pay her for her last two assignments. Even Andre, with his impressive curriculum vita as a lead neuroscientist, could not make enough money to live on.

When Andre returned to the States in 1995 to receive specialized training as an addiction physician, he asked if I could help him get a scholarship for an internship in alcoholism research, so I took him to visit the National Institute of Health (NIH). He was granted a scholarship and he spent several years as an intern in the alcohol research department at Washington University in St. Louis.

He and his wife eventually immigrated to the United States.

Russian Mafia

In the early 1990s, a mafia-led black-market underground economy became the new Russia. Many were alcoholics, especially evidenced by the behavior of Yeltsin, who had stood on a tank to declare that Communism was dead and Russia would now be a democracy. But his alcoholism disease finally destroyed any ability he had to govern and Putin was waiting in the wings to take over. Hopes for democracy dissolved.

The new businessmen and women imploring us to purchase their trinkets surrounded us when we got off buses to visit museums in St. Petersburg, in my first two trips to Russia. Every weekend, residents took their household possessions and found a spot on a street to make some money to survive. Gypsies used babies to con any coins they could by begging on city streets. Some stole my wallet from my fanny pack by cornering me at a subway entrance. Even today, if an enterprising Russian businessman or businesswoman wants to set up a shop to sell or start a charity in new Russia, that person has to pay a bribe to the government official who supervises that district or town.

On one of my trips, I sent a container of donated computers and clothes. When the container arrived, customs officials would not release it without us paying their fee (bribe). In the two weeks I was in Moscow, the container stayed inaccessible to us at the airport. Katja, who then worked for the Salus Foundation as a translator and counselor, spent the whole time I was in Moscow and a month after I had returned home negotiating with the customs officials. Finally, she was able to negotiate the cost of the bribe down enough for them to release the container filled with clothes for an orphanage and used donated computers for a newly established orthodox school.

Con men and crooks, former KGB operatives, now were the new oligarchs.

And the Russian Orthodox Church clerics have been no exception, especially when it came to the import and export business of vodka. My suspicions about Father Irinarch and his delegation proved correct. Not only did he not intend to start an alcohol rehabilitation center in his church, but he benefitted by his contact with Americans to secure needed funds and equipment to rebuild his church building.

Once Putin became president, he and the Russian Orthodox patriarch held regular meetings on important matters. Like the old Russia, no separation of church and state exists. The newly resurrected Russian Orthodox Church prelates, mostly conservatives, are still suspicious of western ways. At first, they believed that the 12-Steps of recovery from alcoholism support groups were cults, just as Protestant Christian missionary church plants were cults. While for a period of time tolerated, nondenominational and denominational new churches are still often considered illegitimate Christianity.

When the evidence of newly sober parishioners proved that the 12-Step way to lifelong recovery works, the Russian Orthodox Church priests began to embrace the spiritual, mental, and social way of healing from the disease of addiction, even supporting the founding of new treatment centers.

Christianity Rises

"Praise to the Lord, Rejoice! He is Risen! He is Risen indeed!" rang out the chorus. The acoustics of the vaulted ceiling and ancient stone walls picked up the song, carrying it as if on angels' wings toward visiting tourists.

As the heavenly music rose and swelled, we peacemakers climbed the stairs of the recently opened St. Basil's Cathedral in Red Square. There, in front of a golden iconostasis, assembled a group of young singers from a Mennonite choir in Lancaster, Pennsylvania. Our joyous hearts, joined by many unseen witnesses, were caught up in the significance of that moment. Out of the suffering of many martyrs, the Church of Christ was rising victorious. Their suffering had not been in vain. One more sacred building confiscated and desecrated by the Communists arose once again as a place for worship.

On my trip in 1992, I met a school teacher named Tatyana and gave her one of my *Tree of Life* books. She told me on a later trip that when she read my book, she became a believer, following her husband, Volodia, who had become a believer a year before her. "His calling," he told me, "is to replace the crosses that were removed from our churches." With a long ladder and his faith in God, the symbolic gold crosses were now reappearing on the tops of the colorful onion domes.

Cross on church

When I visited Tatyana and Volodia again several years later, their son Atrium had started his studies at the Petersburg Orthodox seminary where we had recently stayed.

The Russian Orthodox Church, the largest church in the world, had for a millennium been a strong unifying force within the ebb and flow of the changing Russian politics, remaining eternally changeless in the midst of a changing world. Its religious customs convey the mystical, colorful, emotional, and spiritual mode of eastern Christianity. These eastern Christians have a high tolerance for suffering, for joy, for mystery, for paradox, and for authority. They are otherworldly, having low expectations in this life and noble expectations for eternal life. Their patient Christian witness through forty years of atheistic Communism has been a humbling example of the incarnate, invincible, and eternal Christian faith. They suffered and managed to worship, despite tremendous persecution under Stalin and Brezhnev.

Karl Heim, a German Lutheran theologian, scientist and writer, recorded the first Christian witness under atheistic Communism. He recounted an incident that occurred in Moscow shortly after the Lenin-led revolutionaries seized control from Czar Nicholas II. One of many mass communist meetings was taking place. The leader announced that anyone would be allowed to speak. Many speeches declaring about the glories of Communism were delivered. When all the speeches were concluded, the leader asked if anyone wished to speak about the other side. A small, undernourished priest climbed the stairs. He was reminded by the chairman that he only had five minutes. He replied that he wouldn't need five minutes to say what he had to say. Then he began, "My friends, you have heard all the arguments that have been brought forward to prove the new worldview. But my friends, Christ is risen!" From a thousand voices came back the response: "He is risen indeed, Alleluia."[3]

However, freedom of speech did not last very long. The early open-meeting democracy reverted to a kind of central autocracy. For more than 1,450 years, first under the princes, then under the Shahs and Khans of the Mongols, then under the Czars, the Soviet people knew only a centralized form of government. The Communist Revolution, as a reaction to the wealth and indulgences of the established Orthodox Church, espoused atheism and tried to do away with all religions. Stalin tried to liquidate both religion and morality in the Soviet Union. Mother Russia devoured and enslaved all its neighboring nationalities. Anatoly Lunacharsky, the commissar for education in 1933, stated that Christians must be considered the worst of enemies.[4] Christians between 1929 and 1943 lived the Way of the Cross. The Soviet regime took the lives of forty-two thousand priests and closed five hundred of the six hundred churches in Moscow alone. By 1941, ninety-eight out of every one hundred Orthodox churches no longer existed. The government had either destroyed church buildings or turned them into museums and factories. Many evangelical leaders were shipped off to Siberia to slow death by starvation and torture.[5]

Protestant sects, primarily Baptist, Lutheran, Armenian Apostolic, and Methodist, had coexisted with the Russian Orthodox Church before Communism tenuously at best.

In spite of atheistic Communism, Christianity survived, in both the clandestine meetings of the All-Union Council of Evangelical Christian Baptists and the Russian Orthodox Church.

At the end of World War II, Roosevelt, Churchill,[6] and Stalin, together at Yalta, divided Germany and deeded Eastern Europe over to Communist dictatorship. While the rest of the Western world mesmerized themselves in the atrocities of the Holocaust, Stalin deported millions of peoples in the Baltic countries to forced labor camps after annexing Estonia, Latvia, and Lithuania. There the atrocities paralleled those in Hitler's concentration camps. The same acts of mass deportation and killing took place in Hungary and Czechoslovakia in the 1950s and 1960s.[7]

While staying at the Petersburg Religious Academy, I had an opportunity to read some of the Samizdat literature of the persecuted church describing what it was like for Christians under Communism. Zoya Krakhmalnikova, a journalist, had revived the traditional Christian reading, known as *Nadezhda*(Christian Reading), and collected written letters and testimonials from clerics and religious leaders, then smuggled them to the West. In her book, *Cry of the Spirit, Witnesses to Faith in the Soviet Union*, Tatiana Goricheva chose several letters that had been translated into German and then translated in English by Susan Cupitt.[8] Their letters reflect the tranquility and humility of the inner world of these Christian martyrs.

Anatoly Shurakovski, one of these priests, had been in a forced labor camp for six years when he wrote. He never complained in his letters, he only explained. Writing from the barren, frozen wastelands of Siberia from places such as Svirilag, Solovki, Parandovo, Sonsnovets, Tunguda, Nadvoitsky, Lake Uros and Uroska, he thanked his parishioners for his warm boots, for books, for an icon that focused his prayer life. He described the monotonous round-the-clock labor, which changed often. Sometimes he worked as a statistician, sometimes as a woodcutter, sometimes as a chemist, and sometimes as a guard. He expressed his appreciation when occasionally he was able to sleep in an upper bunk with no bunkmate. Never losing his faith, he read the assigned liturgical prayers, envisioning himself in a church setting. He died slowly with TB, and after being injected with arsenic when he was forty-two years old.

In 1987, two years before I took my first trip to Russia, Russian Orthodox Church leaders had asked Western church leaders to help prepare for the Millennium celebration. The year 1988 would mark the one-thousand-year anniversary of the formal baptism of the Eastern Slavs into Byzantine Christianity. Prince Valdimir, moved by the beauty and mystery of the Orthodox worship service when he visited Constantinople, converted to that faith. Since that time, AD 988, Christianity has had a profound influence on the history of both Russia and Ukraine. Recognizing the importance of that event in the life of Russian people, the Communist government with the Russian Orthodox Church planned a commemorative event to take place in June and July of 1988. Even Mikhail Gorbachev, an avowed atheist (but baptized by his babushka), got caught up in the activities. He stated at that time, "Our main job is to lift the individual spiritually, respecting his inner world and giving him moral strength."[9]

Millennium Memorial

Those who attended the celebrations, both Russian Orthodox and Western religious leaders, believe this Millennium celebration was significant in the breaking up of the Communist empire. Although I wished I could, I was not able to attend that year.

Now the old church buildings are resplendent with their colored domes and gold crosses. They became a symbol of the new Russia, reminding all Russians that Christianity never really dies and rewarding all those like Marie Elizabeth, who had kept the faith alive for so many years. For the first ten years or so, the rebirth of the church became the rebirth of the nation. But restored church buildings did not restore the moral fiber of the Russian people. The priests still were the only ones who could interpret the Scriptures or make God's word come alive.

In 1982, Billy Graham was first invited to give an address to the "World Conference of Religious Workers for Saving the Sacred Gift of Life from Nuclear Catastrophe."[10] The Soviet regime knew that the mainline denominational churches led the Peace movement in the United States. Thus, it was deemed fitting by government officialdom in Moscow to invite a Baptist leader to speak at this conference. Many church leaders in the United States, worried about the propaganda aspects of the trip, warned Billy Graham not to attend. However, he wanted to seize the opportunity to preach the Gospel of Jesus Christ to large audiences. Reluctantly, the Soviet authorities had permitted him to preach in two Moscow churches, as well as speak at the conference. He returned again in 1984, leading the way to the revival of Christianity in the Soviet Union.

In the 1990s, Soviet citizens flocked to be baptized, to read the Bible, and to learn all they could about Christianity. Thanks to an influx of evangelists and church planters, with their message of redemption, justice and peace, house churches became worshipping congregations with newly acquired buildings. How to live a Christian life began to penetrate.

But Russian Orthodox Church leaders criticized the new churches being planted. The Evangelical Baptist Church has been a persecuted minority throughout Russian history. Just as Protestants and Catholics lived side by side for years in the United States with mutual distrust and ridicule, the Russian Orthodox, the Byzantine Catholic, and the Evangelical Baptist Church mutually distrust and are suspicious of one another. Their feudal rivalries are over two hundred years old and wax and wane with the change in political climate.

On September 26, 1997, Patriarch Alexy II became concerned about the growth of new evangelical churches and pushed through the Duma a new law: the Law on Freedom of Conscience and Religious Associations. Under the law, religious associations not registered since 1982 needed to register every fifteen years and only Russians would have the right to form these new associations. Then in July 2017, Putin approved a package of laws restricting missionary activity and evangelism.[11] These laws include not being allowed to share your faith in homes, online, or anywhere else except church buildings.

Once again will there be mass persecution or killing of believers? What will happen to my Russian friends?

PART V

Memorable Musings

Lessons for Today

We were God's enemies, but he made us his
friends through the death of his Son.

ROMANS 5:10A NEB

HAS THERE BEEN A DIFFERENCE in Russian/American relations since the
1980s? What difference have I made? What about the threat of nuclear
war? What about the alcohol and drug problem?

History Repeating Itself applies to Russian/American relations. Once
again, two superpowers have resumed their "undeclared war."

When Communism collapsed, Americans thought we had won the war. Yet, the Russian people, while shamed and humiliated, could now decide their future. They wanted either Communism (the elderly) or the glamorous days of the Czars to return.

Since the Revolution of 1991, some of the Russian people have carried over from their years under Communism fear and distrust of foreigners as well as feelings of being humiliated. Never knowing the value or messiness of democracy, they gravitated back to what was familiar—trusting in a leader, someone like a Czar or a Soviet Secretariat—to take care of them.

Graft and corruption remain unchecked. With no one to guide them except the KGB trained, they have survived and some have thrived with new businesses, while tolerating bribery and dictatorship, just as they had done in the past. Proud and technologically savvy Russians have now taken the lead in cyber technology.

In the United States, we have succumbed to a takeover by the military/industrial powerful lobbyists and corporate interest groups. Our very democratic way of life is at stake. Russia has hacked and manipulated our most recent election. As a result, our new president won the electoral college vote and has introduced a Putin-influenced kleptocracy. Prayer and prophetic persistence, protests, along with repentance, and maybe rebellion might save us.

The threat of nuclear war and resulting nuclear winter is greater than it has ever been. In spite of attempts at nuclear-arms deals and trying to stall and prevent countries such as Iran and North Korea from employing them, visions of new mushroom clouds still hover over the heads of all people on earth. According to a recent *Bulletin of the Atomic Scientists*,[12] fourteen thousand nuclear weapons exist between Russia and the United States. Two thousand of them are on hair-trigger alert. Of all nuclear weapons in the world, our two countries own 905 of them, and both sides talk of building up their arsenals, not tearing them down. More dangerous still is when, where, or whether impulsive Trump, calculating Putin, or malevolent Kim Jong Un will decide to make the first strike.

Some speculate that the current rise in the deaths of young people to alcohol or opiate addictions could be a result of the looming mushroom cloud over their heads. Perhaps, generational brain damage from the abuse of alcohol and pain pills by their parents could be a factor. Perhaps, cultural acceptance, clever advertising, or peer pressure to belong have an influence. Perhaps, neither our government nor the Russian government has provided enough funding for prevention and treatment. Even Zebra's three-year funding has ended. Perhaps, both our countries have fallen away from God. After all, recovery has proven that all it takes is a willingness to turn back to God.

Besides the enveloping crisis of alcohol and opiate epidemics and the threat of nuclear war, Russia rages a cyber war for world dominance and the undermining of Western democracies. Before the rest of the world had caught on, the Russian government under Putin had a monopoly on transmission of fossil fuels and had mastered cyber security with hacking essentials. No agreed-upon rules of engagement exist for cyber warfare. According to the current status of this type of warfare, Russia has the lead.

Regardless of the above threats, both Russian and American people can make a difference individually and collectively. Succumbing to fatalism, disinterest, of dwelling on causes and not solutions will only have disastrous consequences.

I have one last story to share.

"*Zachem* (why)?" Olga asked.

Olga, one of the three Russian parliamentary leaders visiting the United States at the invitation of Peace Links, posed the question to me near the close of a visit with leaders in the prevention and education of families of at-risk children in Pittsburgh. Our meeting took place at the headquarters of the Pittsburgh Leadership Foundation, a foundation whose motto was to make Pittsburgh as famous for Christ as it had been for steel. Each of our visitors—Olga Bessolova, Tamara Leta, and Marina Salye—received corsages of flowers, one red rose, one orchid with a black bow, and one white Easter Lily. We welcomed them with our traditional lunch of sandwiches, coffee and tea, with strawberries and cake for dessert.

Their questions kept coming:

"How come the Holocaust happened?"

"How come Jews and blacks are persecuted?"

"How come someone becomes an alcoholic or a drug addict?"

"How come we destroy our environment?"

"How come we continue to build and test nuclear weapons?"

I thought about the history and culture of the various nationalities of peoples who were enslaved by Communism. I thought about all the wonderful Russian persons I had met and their struggles toward becoming new Russians. I thought about Hiroshima, Nagasaki, Chernobyl, and Three Mile Island.

After what seemed like an eternity, I responded, "Because of Evil. Because sometimes even the best-intentioned ideas, such as the equality of all people, gets corrupted."

"How does one tell the difference between sin and evil?"

We continued the dialogue on the way out the door.

"They are both deceptive," I replied. "Evil is characterized by lies and manipulation of people. Sin is when we turn away from God and think we can do it ourselves. Sin leads to doing evil."

Making a difference only involves a willingness to surrender to God and go forward, no matter what the suffering, no matter what others might say or do to you.

This has been my journey, my song, my willingness to go where God has sent me. There has been suffering along the way—there always is. Have I made a difference? I believe I will be judged by my faithfulness to God's call and my care for God's people.

Maybe some Russian family members have found hope and help in family member support groups. Perhaps, those who have read my book, *Tree of Life,* have become Christians and found recovery. I'll never know how many. All I know is that now I have some Russian friends and colleagues. All I know is that I am not afraid of them and they are not afraid of me. Best of all, there are now 320 Alcoholics Anonymous meetings in fifteen Russian cities, 265 Al-Anon (family member), and ten Alateen groups throughout Russia. God is in the midst of all his people, forgiving, restoring, and healing.

My friends in Russia are praying for us, and we Americans are praying for them.

Lord, let there be peace on earth and let it be because each one of us is making a difference. Alleluia! Amen.

1 Coined by President Ronald Reagan.

2 Boris Segal, *Alcohol Abuse and Alcoholism in the Soviet Union* (New York: Hippocrene Books, 1990).

3 George Carey, *I Believe* (Ridgefield, CT: Morehouse Publishing, 1991), 128.

4 Kent Hill, *The Puzzle of the Soviet Church* (Portland, OR: Multnomah Press, 1989), 92.

5 Ibid., 116.

6 It is interesting to note that Winston Churchill and Franklin Roosevelt's alcohol consumption by this time was well into the addictive stage and thus their cognitive thinking processes were impaired.

7 Popular Front of Estonia, *The Baltic Assembly* (Tartu, Estonia: Valgus Publishers, May 13-14,1989), 8-9.

8   Crossroads, 1989. Texts from fourteen volumes from two bishops and two priests who wrote to their communities, while they were imprisoned, are recorded in this book.

9   Mikhail Gorbachev, *Perestroika: New Thinking for Our Country and the World* (New York: Harper and Row, 1988), 16.

10 A full account of his visit is found in Hill, *The Puzzle of the Soviet Church*.

11 *Christianity Today*, July 17, 2017.

12 Katrina Vanden Heuvel, "Time for Sober Realism on the U.S.–Russia Relationship," *The Washington Post*, July 18, 2017.

AUTHOR BIOGRAPHY

MARY THERESA WEBB IS THE author of *Memories and Miracles: Stories and Reflections on Russians from an American Missionary*; *Who's Calling? Ministry Discernment, Disasters, Restoration*; *Healing Hope for Bruised Souls*; *Healing for Codependent Family Roles*; *Codependence in Family Systems*, and *Tree of Life: The Grace of God and Addiction Recovery*. She has also written several articles on Russia and six historical fiction books for children under the name, Terry Webb.

Webb is a certified pastoral counselor with a master's degree in education and a doctorate in family counseling and addiction intervention. She founded the Christian nonprofit GOAL Project, functioning as Global Addiction Recovery Partners, to train pastors and counselors in the United States and worldwide. Webb is also the founder of Conservation Consultants and Peace Links of Pennsylvania. She was featured in the *World Who's Who of Women*. Webb received the *Lancaster New Era*'s Red Rose Award and the Woman of the Year Award from the *Sewickley Herald*.

48733749R00058

Made in the USA
Middletown, DE
27 September 2017